W9-AHR-386

Squirrels

Julie Murray

Peachtree

abdopublishing.com

Published by Abdo Kids, a division of ABDO, PO Box 398166, Minneapolis, Minnesota 55439.
Copyright © 2016 by Abdo Consulting Group, Inc. International copyrights reserved in all countries.
No part of this book may be reproduced in any form without written permission from the publisher.

Printed in the United States of America, North Mankato, Minnesota.

102015

012016

 THIS BOOK CONTAINS
RECYCLED MATERIALS

Photo Credits: iStock, Shutterstock

Production Contributors: Teddy Borth, Jennie Forsberg, Grace Hansen

Design Contributors: Candice Keimig, Dorothy Toth

Library of Congress Control Number: 2015941767

Cataloging-in-Publication Data

Murray, Julie.

 Squirrels / Julie Murray.

  p. cm. -- (Everyday animals)

ISBN 978-1-68080-119-4 (lib. bdg.)

Includes index.

1. Squirrels--Juvenile literature.   I. Title.

599.36--dc23

                    2015941767

Table of Contents

Squirrels

Chad sees a squirrel.

It is in his backyard.

Some squirrels live in trees.

Others live **underground**.

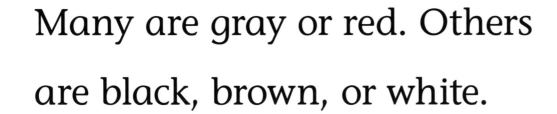

Many are gray or red. Others are black, brown, or white.

They have big eyes.

Their ears are **upright**.

Squirrels climb trees. They use their sharp claws.

They have sharp teeth. They use them to eat nuts.

Many have long, bushy tails.

They use them to balance.

They can run fast.

They can jump far, too!

Have you seen a squirrel?

Features of a Squirrel

eyes and ears

paws and claws

fur

tail

Glossary

underground
beneath the ground.

upright
ears

balance
even out weight to allow one
to stay upright.

upright
raised or standing up.

23

Index

abdokids.com

Use this code to log on to abdokids.com and access crafts, games, videos, and more!

Abdo Kids Code:
ESK1194